PIECES OF ME
A COLLECTION OF POEMS

Maxine Williams Wright

MaxWill
PRODUCTIONS

Where Creativity Comes Alive!

Maxine Williams Wright

MAXWILL PRODUCTIONS, LLC
MARIETTA, GEORGIA 30064

Social Media Platforms
MaxWillPro

www.maxwillproductions.com

info@maxwillproductions.com

Copyright © March 2014 by Maxine Williams Wright

Second Edition February 2024
Pieces of Me published by MaxWill Productions, LLC
Marietta, Georgia 30064

All rights reserved. Professionals and amateurs are hereby warned that the contents are protected under the Copyright Laws of the United States of America and all other countries. No parts of this book can be reproduced in any form or by any means without permission in writing from the publisher.

A certificate was issued under the seal of the Copyright Office in accordance with title 17, United States Code, attests that registration has been made for the work identified with the book Pieces of Me. The information has been made a part of the Copyright Office records.

Book Covers by Lacie Williams
www.custommadeforyou.net

Paperback
ISBN: 978-0-9995249-0-9

Library of Congress: TX 7-814-841 Copyright 2014

Foreword

The poet believes droplets of the unknown are strategically set in motion to cultivate and nourish potential creativity deeply embedded beneath the surface. The delicate flavors in her poems have captured the essence of romance, the sweetness of moments in time, the truth of reality, and the inspiration of faith and hopefulness.

—Dr. Tangela Foster

About the Author

MAXINE WILLIAMS WRIGHT (MAXI)
Playwright, Director, Poet, Actor, Published Author

A native of Memphis, Tennessee enjoys many aspects of performing arts, and her journey started at Northside High School. She continued her education and majored in Theatre and Communications while attending Tennessee State University for three years and obtained her Bachelor of Science from Morris Brown College.

Maxi has a genuine love and concern for the community; she has shared her talents in several capacities for more than 30 years in the Atlanta Metro Area. She has been a member of Turner Chapel AME Church in Marietta, Georgia since 1995. She served as the President of the Drama Ministry from 2012 to August 2019. Maxi received the Taurean Award in May 2019 for director of the 'Best Spiritual Production in 2018' by a Drama Ministry and nominated for 'Outstanding New Playwright in 2018' for the Taurean Award in May 2019. She is grateful for the opportunity to use her creative God given talents. Maxi knows God is always working behind the scenes, with Him "All Things Are Possible."

Maxi is the founder of MaxWill Productions, LLC. The goal of MaxWill Productions is to bring creativity by writing, creating, and producing. MaxWill Productions provides opportunities for actors to use their talents, gain experience, and to have exposure. MaxWill Productions brings quality productions, provides opportunities, and creates platforms for actors, singers, dancers, and technicians. The production company strives to present opportunities for those with a passion for the arts to use their talents.

Where Creativity Comes Alive.

"I Pray with open eyes, I Speak beyond boundary lines, I Write in cyberspace, I Dream of metaphoric rhymes; I… P.S.W.D. with the love I have in me, with the harmony of the Trinity."

Other Works

—Plays—
Down Center
The Corner
Hats
The Manifest

—Books—
FirstBorn (Fantasy, Romance, Horror, Thriller, Mystery)
Toby and Sheba (Children's Literature)
Testimonies, God's Unfolding Miracles (Inspirational)

—Music—
Actuality (Spoken Word)
Georgia Woman, Mississippi Man (Blues Collaboration)

Dedicated To My

Mother & Father
Sons & Grandchildren
Family & Friends

I'm so grateful for the love and support I have received through the years.

Thank You for believing in me, even when I didn't believe in myself.

Table of Contents

Reality

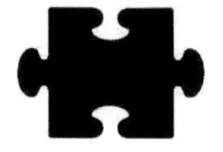

Lift Me Higher 2
Change Is Coming 4
Choices 7
Within 10
Don't Cry For Me 11
Beside Me 13
Our Own 15
There's A Male Child In Our Midst 16
What Do You See 20
Reach 22
Influence 23
I Want To 24
A Vision In The Sky 25
Gonna Tell My Story 26
Take Heed 28
Raised On The Northside 30
Mothers 31
When Can I Call You Dad, Dad 32
The Man In My Life 35
Never Again 37

Inspirational

A Man With Sensitivity 41
Altar Call 44
I- PSWD (Pray ▪ Speak ▪ Write ▪ Dream) 47
It Is Finished 50
Nothing Else To Give 53
Genesis to Revelation 57
My Place 60
Goodness 61
With Him 62
Woman Behold Thy Son 63

MBC

I Have A Revelation For MBC 67
John H. Lewis Gymnasium 69
Wilkes Hall 70
Stance 71
Who's The Man 73
It's All About Helen 74

Moments

If I Could Dance 77
What If 80
When 82
When I Look Back 83
Her Voice 85
Lost 87
Your Presence 88
Juneteenth 89
Now "N" Then 90
Though 91
Enough 92
Once 93
I See 94
They Fought 95
They Have 96
Impact 97
I Wish 98
Bro-Man 99

Romance

Georgia Woman, Mississippi Man 103
Love..105
Is It Real 106
Slow Dance 108
I Can't 110
He Will...111
Hearts..112
Rhythms of the Heart...113

Reality

Lift Me Higher

Oohhh weee, look at the fineness that my eyes have graced upon.
Were you the fantasy between my sheets as I lay with open arms?
Or are you the reality that's here to cause me harm?
Yes, my brother your shoulders look firm and strong enough for a woman of substance.
But will they withstand the encounters of being a Black man.
It takes more than physical strength to lift me higher,
I need to know about all your desires.

You got my attention, but before I give my affection, there are still some things I need to know.

I need to know your expectations of me,
You see,
I'm the type of woman that will stand with you,
By you and for you.
I'll support you,
Comfort you,
And yes,
Love you.
For you to become my King,
You must first treat me like your Queen.
My love is too strong to categorize,
And love such as that will have you mesmerized.
But first,
I must know if you will embrace a monogamous relationship.
Or are you just another brother talking the talk and not walking the walk?

Lying and smiling at the same time while you're trying to
 caress my thighs.
So you can scandalize and dishonor my name.
Naaah my brother,
I'm not falling for that game.

You got my attention, but before I give my affection, I need a bit more information.

The man I need to lift me higher must have a
 relationship with God.
He must know when to fall to his knees to gain the
 spiritual strength needed when going through
 adversities.
I need a man with-
The wisdom of Solomon,
The strength of Samson,
The praise of David,
The radicalness of Malcolm,
The humbleness of Martin,
The sexiness of Denzel,
And the insightfulness of Barack.
Are you that Man?
If not,
Step on with your fine self.
You see,
Today I require much more than physical fineness.

Change is Coming

When change comes,
It makes no introduction, nor does it care about how it's-
Received,
Perceived,
Or if it's believed.
Change can make the-
Impossible - - probable,
Impractical - - sensible,
Irrational - - logical.
Old things shall die,
When the birth of new things arise.
Change brings about a difference in-
Your talk,
Your walk,
Your attitude with new abiding rules.
Change is coming when you go from-
Ordinary to extraordinary,
Discrimination to justification,
Isolation to collaboration,
Frustration to compensation.

It's been a long time coming– I'm ready for my change– it's been proclaimed– I won't be the same.

Change can turn-
Hate to love,
Loneliness to companionship,
Displeasing to satisfying,
Grief to joyfulness.
Change can make the-
Last- to first,
Poor- to rich,

Unemployed- to employed,
A boy- to a man,
An unbeliever- to a believer.
When change is accepted it brings-
Newness,
Insightfulness,
Endless possibilities,
And the right man or woman in your life.
Change can convert-
An apartment to a house,
A boyfriend or girlfriend to a spouse,
An enemy to a friend.

It's been a long time coming– I'm ready for my change– it's been proclaimed– I won't be the same.

Change can also remove opposition and place you in a favorable position.
It can close critical eyes,
Silence judgmental tongues,
And release you from self-inflicted bondage.

Change can place-
An African American in the White House,
Citizens throughout this land gather around a table to discuss issues at hand to empower this nation.
Change can put-
God in your life,
Relieve you from strife,
Remove apprehension with His shield of protection,
Then make everything alright.
Change is coming-
Examine the reflection that you cast,
Remove the weeds,

Plant new seeds,
Offer honorable deeds,
Step through your open door and receive- your change.

It's been a long time coming— I'm ready for my change— it's been proclaimed— I won't be the same. It's been a long time coming, but change is gonna come— oh yes it will.

Choices

Ahhhh… screamed his mother as she rushed to his side
    as he laid on the street corner.
She watched the blood gush from his head,
Another young brother dead.
As his spirit departed his body,
He knew it was the money and drugs-
That put the bullet in his head that killed him dead.
As he ascended, he heard his mother's screams,
He realized he was the last of her dreams.
She held his lifeless body and said,
Your acceptance letter arrived for College.

Believe in yourself… you have a choice today! What you gonna do after graduation day? Will you talk the talk and walk the walk or will you just be another…

Bang… as the cell door slammed to confine an honor
    roll student.
Got involved with the wrong gang,
Trying to prove he too could be cool.
He heard the cell door slam,
The reality of the twenty-five years ripped through his
    soul,
He hung himself in his jail cell.
As he hung-
Tears streamed down his face,
Another young brother taken from our race,
Committed the crime but not man enough to serve the
    time.

Believe in yourself… you have a choice today! What you gonna do after graduation day? Will you talk the talk and walk the walk or will you just be another…

Ouch… is all she could yell as the baby's head made its
    way on his to-be birthday.
She was only thirteen when a young boy said,
I love you in the dark, in some bushes, in the park.
All she really wanted was to be loved,
She gave her body to feel a hug.
Sex was love-
Love was sex and by the time she was 17,
She had three babies with three different daddies.

Believe in yourself… you have a choice today! What you gonna do after graduation day? Will you talk the talk and walk the walk or will you just be another…

Smcchh… took them beyond their consciousness as they
    sucked on a pipe with all their might.
Too many puffs enslaved them to an addiction beyond
    their own recognition.
They had been Homecoming King and Queen-
Lived in the suburbs,
Now no place to call home as they roam the streets
    alone,
Doing whatever it takes to get their next high.
You see…
That's the price you pay when you so dangerously play.

Believe in yourself… you have a choice today! What you gonna do after graduation day? Will you talk the talk and walk the walk or will you just be another…

Choose
'No' to deceitful activity,
'No' to negative influence,
'No' to unproductive association-
That will prevent you from being placed amongst the
    stars.
Believe in yourself and in God,
You shall overcome all barriers that stand in your way,
You shall overcome abusive circumstances.
Believe that you have royal blood in your veins,
You have been destined to achieve,
Destined to rule…
Destined to lead…
Destined to be somebody…

Believe in yourself… you have a choice today! What you gonna do after graduation day? Will you talk the talk and walk the walk or will you just be another…

Within

Why must you continue to compete with me?
I'm drained from the self-inflicted agony of countless
    attacks,
I will remain intact.

You will not win,
I will not pretend,
Will mend-
Not depend on sins of the skin.
I'm the inner and you're the outer,
Victory from within.

Don't Cry for Me

Wipe your eyes so all the world can see just how
    wonderful you were to me.
In your eyes I saw the light,
They aided me through the darkness of many long
    unbearable nights.
I needed your eyes for I saw the love within them,
Which helped me through that cycle of my life.

So, don't cry for me,
You see I'm pain free and not only can I stand again,
I can soar like never before.

Your arms were used to embrace me,
Guide me, comfort me.
The love within your arms gave me power,
Confidence, the will to live.
Your arms provided me with-
Hope when I was hopeless,
Strength when I was weak,
Courage when I was afraid.

So, don't cry for me,
Now I am the man I used to be…
You would be so very proud of me…
You see I'm standing before royalty.

I will be waiting,
Then we will have all eternity,
You have many more years before your journey is over.
God has more work for you to do,
There are other souls that need you.

Just remember God is a whisper away,
He will catch every tear that falls from your face,
He will kiss your eyes as you sleep through the night,
So they will continue to be a source of light for those
    that need your insight.

He will strengthen your arms through the stillness as you
    sleep,
Empower them for the souls you are yet to meet.
Now you are ready to become the force which you were
    designed to be.
I am thankful God blessed me with thee.

Don't cry for me,
My journey is over,
His grace and mercy granted my one request,
To have my loved ones together again,
Now I Can Rest.

Beside Me

Come and take your place beside me,
Not in the front or behind-
By my side with thee.

Let us take this journey together as man-
As woman.
I'll be the support for your shoulders,
When your arms are burdened with despair.

Even during moments of weakness-
You are strong.

What God instilled in you is like no other…
My brother.

Now come take your place beside me.
We will navigate this journey as father and as mother.

You can offer your fatherly traits to the fatherless,
While I offer my motherly traits to the motherless.

Nurturing seeds that we did not plant,
Knowing the seeds will be the birth of a new nation.

The prayers,
The tears,
The sacrifices will be glorified with the new harvest.

Oh come take your place beside me,
Show me how to be the anchor for your existence,
The foundation for your steps.

I'll be there with you-
For you-
Beside you.

I'll place my hands around your hands to form a firm
    grip that will hold your life.

I need your life to coexist with my life.
Take your place beside me,
As we love each other.

Our Own

Have you ever thought how we can step over a homeless man?
Then go to a foreign land with helping hands.
There are many souls in this land that are astray,
They have nowhere to lay,
No pillows for their heads,
No blankets,
No gas,
No electric,
No plumbing,
Just concrete beds.

We build homes for others in foreign lands,
While family and friends lose their homes to foreclosures on these sands.
We build and fund schools that won't benefit our children,
Yet our schools are closing due to no accreditation,
Leaving our children lacking education.

Take care of home first then quench your thirst.
Offer deeds,
Fall to knees,
Set our people free,
Believe in this humanity.

There's A Male Child In Our Midst

He is right here–
Can't you see him?
Don't ignore him nor pretend not to see or hear his
 cries.
The male child needs you.
Maybe,
He's a male child that you know,
Or the little boy next door.
He is here watching,
Waiting,
Listening,
Praying for someone to reach out to.

The father of the male child does not understand–
His son has not received the one thing that only he can.
The father of this male child is too busy trying to find his
 own way.
He's a child he chooses to forget,
Not support,
Not love,
Not claim,
Isn't that a shame?
If only the father would take the time–
Make an effort to stay in his life,
Make the necessary sacrifice.
This child is your blood,
Your seed,
Your son.
Come back and take your place- secure him in your
 arms.

There's a woman on her knees praying, there's a man in the streets dying, and a child somewhere crying.

The mother of the male child is there with him,
By him,
For him,
Providing-
Teaching-
Always praying.
She sacrifices her dreams,
Ambitions,
Passions.
Her role is both mother and father,
Only her God sustains her.
She lacks the knowledge to rear a male child,
She reaches out to family,
Friends, her church, no one really cares,
She encounters judgmental stares.
The men of her family have no time to help develop,
Lead,
Or assist with her male child,
Fail to realize,
Quick to criticize.
The church members only willing to pray for him,
Too afraid the male child will see the imperfections in
    them.
The parents of the male child's father,
Say he's too dark-
They choose not to understand.
Instead,
They support their son that chooses not to be a man,
Leaving the male child without the wisdom from his
    grandparents' hands.

Is there anybody out there? Is there anybody who cares?
Is there anybody out there? Is there anybody who really cares?

The mother of the male child surrenders,
She cries out.
She falls to her knees-
With a dire plea to her God,
To lead her male child to his rightful deed.
The male child is our future-
Somehow we must reach him,
So we can teach him.
We must let him know that we do love him.
He needs to know that all things are possible.
We must let him know that God is waiting,
Has promised to give him a new beginning,
Instead of a destructive ending.
We must instill in him the belief that he has a place,
Will not be 'the male child in our midst,
Will become 'the male child in His grace'.

There's a woman on her knees praying, there's a man in the streets dying, and a child somewhere crying.

Hear him,
Father of the male child.
Hear his cries,
Feel his anger,
Fill his needs,
Know his desires,
Believe in his dreams.
Be there for him,
It's not too late to step up-
Take your place.

Don't let him slip away into an endless existence that you
 can change.
Give our male child a tomorrow-
Release him from his sorrows.
Standup and claim your role,
Make a difference that's meaningful.
Provide the foundation he can hold on and depend on.
In order for him to become the designed being,
Develop into the King he was born to be,
Believe in thee.
Let our male child lead us,
That we as a race are desperately in need of.
Or you can choose not to care,
There will be a mass deterioration throughout this
 nation.

Is there anybody out there? Is there anybody who cares?
Is there anybody out there? Is there anybody who really cares?

What Do You See

I often wondered what older ladies thought when they looked at me,
As they smiled gracefully with honor and dignity.
Did they reflect on their youthfulness and the foundations they steered?
Did they say she would soon see what it feels like to be me?
Would she embrace the wise lines-
That brought forth power and pride.
Would she embrace the dimple thighs-
That birthed traditions with missions.
Would she embrace the sagging nipples-
That nursed blood lines through moments in time.
Would she embrace the gray thinning hair upon her head,
That provided wisdom through a declining economic system.

What do you see when you look at me?
Do you see the reflection of you in me beneath the surface yearning to be set free?
Knowing what you know now-
Would you do it again differently?
Would you say 'no' when you mean 'no',
'Yes' when you mean 'yes',
To pass your life's test?
Would you know how to rid needless stress-
As you sort through difficultness?
Would you place more value on conditioning your heart and mind-
Instead of rubies and wine?

Would you allocate time for subject matters with
 measures-
Without hidden pleasures?
Would you be able to read between the lines this time-
If given a second chance to take a stance?

Now I know what older ladies thought when they looked
 at me,
Cause now it's me that look and see-
As I smile so gracefully with dignity.
A young girl walked by with her head raised high,
Wearing her hat tilted to the side,
Her jeans hugged her thighs.
I wondered what happened to the time-
When did it pass me by?
Why didn't it allow me to say goodbye?

She looks back at me with a replica expression.
I smile-
Then bow-
Now it's time for you to take center stage.
You too shall know the intricacies when you look and
 see,
But only you won't be looking at me.

Reach

There are so many within arms' reach hurting beneath,
Embrace those within your space.

Feed them filet mignon,
Volume down sad songs,
Forecast our young.

Serve a smile,
A hug,
A conversation,
To stimulate motivation.

Reach-
To stay the course-
Reach-
To deter remorse.

Influence

I stand by classroom doors-
Listening to sounds of seashores.

As waves of feet stagger to seats-
Awaiting unknown expectations to meet.

I aim to pierce the shields of minds,
To influence lifetimes.

I Want To

Tell me NOW how you feel
I want to
Hear your words

I want to
Smell your flowers

I want to
See your expressions

I want to
Feel your emotions

I want to
Absorb it all on this side
Before the glory ride.

A Vision In The Sky

Her lines of time are defined by meaningful rhymes,
She spills her mind.
She embraces the fine lines-
They provide wisdom and pride-
Where loyalty resides.
She produced generations through her channel door,
Each model of none before.
She's the queen bee with bittersweet stings,
She sings upbeat rings refusing routines.

A vision in the sky, purpose by her side, service on her mind, praising the Most High.

Her essence,
Made to withstand the demands of being a spiritual woman.
Her methods are selective with clear perspectives.
Her love stretches across the sands of time beyond boundary lines.
Her touch will regulate your pulse with meaningful results.
Her gaze is able to penetrate souls-
Release truths untold.
Her voice is melodic, undertone is hypnotic.
Don't let her smooth sound deceive you.
She appears meek, wearing her sleek physique,
Yet, she'll ride or die for her peeps,
It's best to stay on the safe side of her street.

A vision in the sky, purpose by her side, service on her mind, praising the Most High.

Gonna Tell My Story

Take a seat my child and rest your feet,
I need you to listen for a while before I rock myself to sleep,
Want to share the hearts of mothers to thee.

God made Mothers like no other,
Serum of a four-leaf clover,
Heaven's undercover.
There's no mystique about their reasoning or their blend of seasoning.
Their formations define perpetual rhymes,
Their lips speak trumpet lines-
Emancipating minds.
They plant seeds of spirituality to nourish families,
They declare the prayer of Jabez on generations to be.
They counteract wavering beats conquering defeats with no retreat.

Sing your song child,
Oh, I'll be awhile…
Gonna tell my story before I go to glory.
Gonna tell my grandchildren of my chariot ride,
While praising the Most High.

God gave Mothers firm backs to encounter attacks,
Knowing when to react,
Retract or accept undeniable facts.
Mothers are made to withstand the hands they were dealt-
Staying true to self.
Mothers have hearts that circulate love,
Used to channel little ones to glory above.

Their love stretches across the sands of time beyond painful lines,
They seek soundless nursery cries.
Their touch will regulate your pulse with meaningful results.
Their gaze is able to penetrate perceptions–
Expose misinterpretations.
Their recipes bring lost souls' home,
Consume unsettled undertones.

Sing your song child,
Oh, I'll be awhile…
Gonna tell my story before I go to glory.
Gonna tell my grandchildren of my chariot ride,
While praising the Most High.

Take Heed

It's time to rejoice,
To turn-up the noise
To yell and tell
To dance about
To unsilence your mouth.
Still got oil in this engine,
Did I mention the food cooked in the kitchen?
I love to blend recipes and things
To taste the meanings
To keep it interesting
To create new happenings.
Don't have time to pout
I got too many reasons to shout.
Too blessed to stress
No time for mess
Too busy trying to pass this test
Shall put forth my best to excel the rest beyond the next.

> *Take heed to what I say on this day*
> *Got wisdom I want to share to make you aware.*
> *I want to take my grandchildren by their hands*
> *Teach them to understand the conception of man*
> *To follow plans without complicated demands.*

Got this pattern I want to sew
To warm souls for temperatures below zero.
This shoelace I want to tie
To keep feet from tripping by.
This nose I want to wipe
So lungs can breathe insight.
This bedtime story I want to tell
Cause dreams are not for sale.

This lullaby I want to sing
So ears can depict melodies as they ring.
This dance I want to learn
To teach progression when steps are firm.
This hug I want to give
To show the difference between fake and real.
To let them know the plight will come during the cycle of life
How it's handled determines the honorable stripes.
Do you see my smile?
Carried me through subliminal miles with style.
Do you see my stand
I know I'm a woman not a man
I hold the Lord's hand as I kneel to accept His divine plan.

Take heed to what I say on this day
Got wisdom I want to share to make you aware.
I want to take my grandchildren by their hands
Teach them to understand the conception of man
To follow plans without complicated demands.

Raised on the Northside

Though I walk through the valley of the shadow of death.
I will not fear as God is with me guiding my steps.
Raised on the northside.
Running from bullies on my backside.
A girl without ties unsure of tomorrow's sorrows.
Mama taught me how to fight to survive.
Threw me outside when I was running from five.
Had to win to stay alive.
Ain't no woman could touch her.
She stood 5 feet with Ali's fists.
My strength came from her toughness.
I don't care if I'm not in your click.
Now, I don't fight I just write.
He clears my path with His light.

Mothers

This is a day that All can recognize-
The essence
The beauty
The strength
The endurance
The love
The spirit of a Woman.

We, the mothers of the present have not forgotten the sacrifices of the mothers of the past.
The mothers that held the torch that guided the mothers of today-
To light
To victory
To our Savior.

The mothers of the past that instilled-
Faith
Resilience
Aspiration
Which we,
The mothers of today will extend to the mothers of tomorrow.

Being a Woman is being a Mother
We have steered paths
Touched hearts
Enlightened spirits of those that have encountered
Our substance
Our wisdom
Our grace.

When Can I Call You Dad, Dad

When can I call you dad, dad?
Was it the time you chose to leave and not say goodbye,
While I was in the arms of the woman that you made
    cry?

Or was it when you promised that you would visit and
    take me to my favorite place?
I fell asleep on the porch 'because I had waited all day.
Then mom carried me to bed,
Kissed the dried tears upon my face.

As I blew out my birthday candles,
I wished for you to come to my party,
Not knowing whether you had forgotten-
Or didn't want to be bothered.

When I played my first little league football game,
I kept searching for your face in the crowd,
Man– I wanted you to see me when I made my first
    touchdown.

Then the years kept going by-
You didn't come by to say Hi,
My love and hurt turned to anger,
I started not to care about the danger.

But when I looked in the eyes of the one who was there
    as a mother and a father,
I knew I had caused hurt to the one person I loved like
    no other.

I stopped feeling sorry for myself-

Learned that through knowledge I would excel,
And to appreciate the grace that God had given to me as well.

I whispered a prayer for you,
To make all your dreams come true,
I prayed that you would find your place as you go through.

I'm not a little boy anymore,
Time has made me so much more,
Now I can see the struggles you went through-
As this world got the best of you.

Now it's time for me to take my place as I walked across this stage,
I received high honors that day,
But will I continue to engage?

Mom did the very best she knew how,
Even when she couldn't figure me out,
She never gave up,
She knew I was the child created by you.

Now you've found your place,
Don't be afraid to come and claim your space,
We have been here the entire time,
Longing to see your face.

There will always be a place in my life for you,
Now I have a son too,
When I see his little face,
That's all I need to help me make it through this race.

And when he calls me Dad,
I often think of you,
Wanting to call you that too,
It's okay if you come around,
I think Granddad will fit you.

Mom comes around quite often,
That's what you do when you are family,
When I watch them together,
It makes me remember,
How we used to be when we were together.

The Man In My Life

I look in your eyes-
I can see the frustration yet the determination,
That makes our family unit have a solid foundation.

Because if it were not for you,
We would not be complete,
You provide the final touch we seek.

The man you are, is the man I hope to be,
Because you can work hard all day,
Still have the strength to play with me.

Dad, I love you so much, but my little lips cannot say the
    words yet,
I know you can tell,
By the way I hug you until.

I want the entire world to know my Dad is the best,
He's better than all the rest.

You always find the time to support me,
Help me,
Comfort me,
I strive to be all I can be.

My legs are stronger now-
Can carry me like a man,
As I stand by your side,
Like father,
Like son,
We are the same inside.

You instilled in me the knowledge of self-worth,
And I'm so proud I had you all to myself.

Because of you,
I will be able to achieve my dream,
It is an honor to be on your team.

I remember you whispering in my ear before I fell asleep
    each night,
How important it is not to give up the fight,
Try with all your might.

As a man now,
I stand firm from following your teachings,
I'm able to obtain my mission.

Never Again

In the morning when I open my eyes from a restful night,
See the sun as it shines.
And when I look at the sky at night,
See the moonlight when it's full bright,
Think about what lovers do when the mood is right,
Allow my heart to get lost in the midnight.

What... or should I say-
When I woke up this morning-
Looked in the mirror-
Saw another line upon my face,
Which is quite fine.

But what did I do in-between that time of that line?
Did I extend a helping hand to aid a friend-
Or was I somewhere committing a sin?
Did I let my light so shine-
Or was I too drunk with wine?
Did I provide a source for the blind-
Or I didn't have the time?
Did I assist a mother with five in the welfare line-
Or did I ignore her cries?
Did I provide shelter to the homeless-
Or did I walk on by?
Did I care for the sick-
Or was I selfish?

Be careful what you say, be careful what you do... it just might come back on you.

All I can say is never again shall I ignore the tears,
The hurt-
The suffering endured by my sister-
How could I not see her pain- was I inhumane?

Never again shall I-
Look and not see,
Hear and not listen,
Talk and not speak,
Bend and not stand,
Crawl and not walk,
God made me a Woman- not a Man,
He gave me the substance within my breasts to nurse a nation.

Never again shall I complain about much of anything,
You see...
God has kept me from-
Being homeless and sleeping on the streets,
Having an addiction I can't beat,
Selling my body to eat,
From many unknown defeats.

Never again shall I eat without praying for those that are less fortunate than me,
There are women and children throughout this land that are hungry right now as I speak.

Be careful what you say, be careful what you do... it just might come back on you.

Never again shall I,
Think time has settled my debt,
Forget favors that were God sent,

Not appreciate my many strengths,
Witness suffering and not offer comfort,
Dismiss love sent from above,
Be unkind to those that are not in their right mind,
Let fear of failure keep me confined,
Allow a person or situation make me-
Fuss,
Cuss,
And not trust,
Lie when I should testify,
Exploit my body for unrighteous disorder.

And never again…
Shall be engraved this day forth,
When you're over fifty,
You have a brand-new perspective.

Be careful what you say, be careful what you do… it just might come back on you.
Be careful what you say, be careful what you do… you don't know who's watching you.

Inspirational

A Man with Sensitivity

I've watched you from the time you were submerged,
Held you close when you didn't have the nerves.
For years we were a team,
Just you and I against all means.
You released My hand to conquer other demands–
Not in our plans,
I captured the snares of the world as they were hurled.

I was the best man when you said, "I do"
Even when I told you– not to.
I believed the vision in your eyes,
The dash in stride,
As you strategized,
Ride or die with you when the vision didn't materialize.

You need a man with sensitivity– that man is Me– can't you see– trust and believe in Me.

I didn't have the charms to keep you in My arms,
Nor the admirations to stimulate your sensations.
Placed on a shelf to collect dust,
As you rushed into another affiliation that lacked
    substance for a loving relation.
I stayed in My place–
Kept an eye on you–
Even when you didn't want Me to.
I told My Father, I couldn't give up on you–
In your heart I knew you loved Me too.
You had faith in Me to-
Defuse when you were misused,
Abused, left confused.

You need a man with sensitivity– that man is Me– can't you see– trust and believe in Me.

One morning I knocked on your door,
I turned to walk away like I had many times before.
I heard you yell My name,
I hastened to your side–
Glorified with pride–
Jubilant to reside inside–
Your heart.
You stepped into the realm of My hem by the way of My stem.
You embraced Me–
I fell to My knees as you touched Me.
A layer of your skin fell dead,
As a reptilian would shed.
You urged–
To emerge into an electric surge.
We confessed our unreserved love with purified blood.
My love has always been more than physical,
It is spiritual.
I've loved you more than you could ever imagine with infinite passion.

You need a man with sensitivity– that man is Me.

I was born to love you.
I left My home for you.
I traveled the roads in search of you.
I was baptized for you.
I fed five thousand for you.
I raised the dead and healed the sick for you.
I prayed 40 days and 40 nights for you.
I was betrayed and denied for you.

I sacrificed Myself for you.
I wore a crown of thorns for you.
I was crucified for you.
I rose the third day for you.
I ascended back to My Father for you.
I sent My Holy Spirit to be with you.
I Am the Word,
And I will never leave you.

I Am the Man with Sen-Si-Tiv-I-Ty!

Altar Call

As you enter the place of worship you make sure all eyes are on you,
As you strut your stuff to your favorite pew.
You brought with you the same condescending attitude that seems to follow you.
As you position yourself to listen to the message,
You received a text from your date,
Telling you not to be late for the rendezvous you have with him at half past two.
Your Pastor speaks about the Virtuous Woman,
Which gets your attention,
The sermon seems to give you some tension.
As he continues to deliver his message there's a sense of uneasiness,
Your spirit just won't let you rest.
A spirit of conviction comes over you,
Then the presence of the Holy Spirit surrounds you.
You jump to your feet and move them to a Holy Ghost beat.
As you walk from the pew to the altar,
Your heart is heavy,
Your tears are plenty as you recall your sinful journey.
Your sin sick soul cries out-
Just like that-
The weight of your sins become lighter,
With every step you take toward the altar.

This is an altar call for the mothers, daughters, sisters... fall to your knees, and set your burdens free. Fall to your knees and rise to your destiny.

While at the altar you are freed from the judgment you
 made on the mother with five,
The choice you made not to keep yours alive.
He freed you from the men you played,
You paid-
The souls you could have saved.
He freed you from the lies you told,
The sex you sold,
The drugs you used up your nose.
He freed you from the hate embedded in your heart,
The thoughts that kept you lost.
He freed you from-
Envy, jealousy, hostility, animosity, rivalry,
So you could become the Virtuous Woman you were
 meant to be.
He freed you from your sin-stained sheets,
Rather it was for-
Gratification,
Classification,
Ratification.

This is an altar call for the mothers, daughters, sisters… fall to your knees, and set your burdens free. Fall to your knees and rise to your destiny.

As you are down on your knees you are revived and
 purified by His love,
Cleansed and redeemed by His blood.

He wants you to-
Be like Mary- Mother of Jesus,
Be faithful to Him despite it all,
No matter what you are called.

Be like Ruth-
Be willing to forsake your ethnic ways-
Follow God,
He will make it worth your while each and every day.

Be like Abigail-
Be wise and aware of your surroundings-
Generous to those that do evil unto you,
He will bring deliverance upon you.

Be like Anna-
Serve God not only by day,
But by night,
His presence will be with you throughout your life.

Be like Deborah-
Pour out your heart onto the Lord,
He will shower His blessings upon you like a waterfall.

Be like the sinner woman that-
Washed, wiped, kissed, anointed His feet,
Through her faith she was saved,
When He extended His grace.

This is an altar call for the mothers, daughters, sisters...fall to your knees, and set your burdens free. Fall to your knees and rise to your destiny.

Now go and sin no more...
God will be with you forever more,
Trust in the Lord with all thine heart,
He shall restore.

I -P.S.W.D. (Pray•Speak•Write•Dream)

The reflection from her disenchanted eyes show
    incompletes,
Defeats,
Acts of retreat,
Live your life free of negativity.
If your life is basic,
It's time to elevate it.
Don't listen to superficial talkers that walk with walkers,
Not spiritual enough to step in faith.
They provide temporary solutions as forms of
    resolutions,
Not caring about conclusions.
There's everlasting power in His grace,
Hasten to the steps of His pace,
Step into your destiny with certainty,
Filled with integrity with radiant harmony.
Like a psalmist singing,
Melodies clinging to new beginnings.
Stepping to unwinding positions-
You seize visions for missions.
You step in tune as you inhale revelations of fumes,
That explodes the tomb meant for your doom.
Step to the left,
Step to the right-
Step to avoid the strife in life.

I get lost in time as I search through your manipulated
    mind.
I want you to reconsider before you pull the trigger,
Allow God to reconfigure.
The perplexities of this world shadow you in a realm
    from the lack of the Most High's stem.

Even the woman with the issue of blood knew to touch His hem.

I **P**ray with open eyes,
    I **S**peak beyond boundary lines,
        I **W**rite in cyberspace,
            I **D**ream of metaphoric rhymes,
                I **P.S.W.D.**— *the love I have in me,*
                    With the harmony of the Trinity.

The reflection from his disenchanted eyes show heavy burdens,
Lack of gladden,
Full of sadden,
Believe the promises of heaven.
Your life was once transfused,
Now it's time to defuse.
The grim reaper wants you dead,
He stands beside your bed dressed in black with a touch of red.
Through the window comes the moonlight,
Shines in the midst of darkness with radiant brightness,
Brings into being your new likeness.
I get lost in time as I search through your manipulated mind.
I want you to reconsider before you pull the trigger,
Allow God to reconfigure.

I **P**ray with open eyes,
    I **S**peak beyond boundary lines,
        I **W**rite in cyberspace,
            I **D**ream of metaphoric rhymes,
                I **P.S.W.D.** — *the love I have in me,*
                    With the harmony of the Trinity.

The sins of your tongue swallowed your essence to go
    from beyond,
It has the power of life and death.
You must control what you say,
It can determine your destiny.
Your breakthrough is on the other side,
Buckle-up for your victory ride.
Step into your destiny with certainty,
Filled with integrity with a radiance of harmony.
A new season is stepping into a scope of reason without
    treason.
There's a new perspective when methods are selective.
Drain the malice from your ears-
Heard through the years.
Step to the left,
Step to the right-
Step to avoid the strife in life.

*I **P**ray with open eyes,*
    *I **S**peak beyond boundary lines,*
        *I **W**rite in cyberspace,*
            *I **D**ream of metaphoric rhymes,*
                *I **P.S.W.D.** – the love I have in me,*
                    With the harmony of the Trinity.

It Is Finished

At the beginning I was there-
I saw the disappointment in My Father's eyes,
When His first seeds ate from the forbidden tree.
I knew then it would be Me to make amends,
To bring forth trends.
I prepared Myself for the outcome,
John the Baptist preached of the One to come,
To save the kingdom,
The only way for your redemption.

This journey was planned for you-
Every phase of My earthly life was to bring you insight.
I came to-
Preach,
Teach,
Make disciples of men,
To give the hopeless hope,
To make amends for sins.
Anyone that suffers strife by following My life-
Shall have a reservation in the Book of Life.

I came to do My Father's Work,
I came to show you how much you are loved,
I came to deliver a message from above,
I came to-
Magnify,
Glorify,
Amplify the name of the Most High.
I came to testify if you comply.
I came to defy the enemy thrown from the sky.
I came to carry My cross to keep you from being lost.

I came to wear a crown of thorns so you could be
  adorned.

My work is done-
Have proven My obedience-
The alliance has begun-
The new covenant reigns with purified blood as it runs.

I bow My head-
I Am announced dead as My blood sheds,
Through the dark of red My spirit fled.
The blood that gives everlasting life-
With the absence of birthrights.
The blood that guides lost souls-
From valleys to mountain peaks-
From alleys to highways-
From condemnation to salvation.

The purpose is finished,
The suffering is finished,
The redemption is finished,
This ending leads to new beginnings.
Bringing living water for you to drink at will,
The over-spill of My Holy Spirit shall-
Regulate,
Modulate,
Fulfill.
Now you know the love My Father has for you-
The love I have for you-
The love My Holy Spirit shall bestow upon you.

From dawn to dusk You hung on a cross for the sake of us,
In You we trust our souls to keep as we weep at Your feet.

You paid the highest sacrifice with Your life,
At the cross where I first saw the light.
They hung You high,
Stretched You wide
Pierced You in Your side.
On an old rugged cross that stood on Calvary where my
    Savior died to sanctify thee-
To loosen impurities-
To form the Trinity.

From dawn to dusk You hung on a cross for the sake of us,
In You we trust our souls to keep as we weep at Your feet.

Nothing Else To Give

As I reminiscence about the years of yesterday,
I try to identify on how I reached this place in my life-
All the years I've sacrificed.
Cause now I'm ready to testify.
I'm ready to say 'no' to the relationships only I thought
   were friendships.
No longer will I provide support that's unappreciated
   without being compensated.
I'm ready to take back-
My time,
My dimes,
And my mind.

I have nothing else to give,
I'm drained from the many heart aches that caused this
   pain.
I'm weary,
Worn,
Scorned from the thorns in my back.
I'm tired of giving love-
And not receiving any from those that want plenty.
I'm tired of giving to the takers that are baby makers.
I'm tired of the haters,
But I use them as motivators.
I'm tired of the hypocrisy in my church ministries caused
   by iniquities.
I'm tired of the injustice in the judicial systems that
   enslave our men in captivity,
Leaving their women and children in disparity.
I'm tired of the illegal immigrants that work toward no
   pensions,
Leaving the US citizens in omission.

I'm tired of companies sending jobs overseas-
When there are mouths here to feed.
I'm tired of the wasted years,
Wasted tears due to my fears.
And now you say to me,
I must sustain in order to take my claim that's ordained.
Father, You say to me,
I'm in Your plans,
You want me to continue to believe,
Trust and work for You.
You will reward my labor,
Stamp Your seal,
Confirm the deal,
Make all my dreams real.
But Father, I have nothing else to give.

God said, yes my child, I know your every pain,
I will supply you with the strength you need to maintain.
I want you to call My name and get closer to Me as you
    continue your journey.
I recognized your endless labor,
I gave you time to rest,
During that time I made sure all your needs were met.
I pruned,
Tuned,
And refined.
Multiplied your dimes thousands of times,
Revived your mind so you could write these rhymes.
Now, I ask you,
Do you still have nothing else to give-
Or should I say My child be still as I unfold past
    miracles.

The years you chose not to obey and walked not by My side.
I told Gabriel to blow his horn to release the multitude of angels from beyond,
To cover you from the rising of the sun 'til the going of the same.
I knew you were confused,
Yet ashamed when you chose not to worship My Name.
I waited with open arms-
Extended hands,
You were in My plans.
After many wasted years you returned to My domain,
You needed shelter from the rain-
To wash away your stains.
I blew the winds upon your face to dry your tears,
To loosen your fears.
I carried you through the storms-
Not a scratch on you was formed.
I relieved you from strife-
Endured the sacrifice.
I kissed your cheeks while you were asleep,
Placed a shield of protection from your head to your feet.
Now do you still have nothing else to give?

Oh Father, forgive me for all my ungratefulness.
I kneel before you on bended knees,
Will testify to love received.
Thank You for my life and Your insight.
Thank You for Your shield of protection,
When I was headed for self-destruction.
Thank You for the footprints in the sand-
When I couldn't stand.
I will give my time,

My dimes,
And my mind.
I will plant a harvest of new seeds,
Will produce a crop of noble deeds.
I Have Everything to Give–
My Labor Shall Exceed!

Genesis to Revelation
Collaboration with Austin T. Wright

The beginning,
With four words,
Let there be light.
It was destined,
The trees,
The breeze,
The seas,
Mother earth's very essence-
Such a work of art scoped to perfection.

Was it enough,
Or room for one more blessing?
A vision,
A creation with such precision,
Designed by His own divine image,
To whom this would all be given,
Beasts big and small would all listen.
He took the clay of the earth-
Shaped man- from man shaped woman.
Men, women, and children to live with no worries,
Proven to be unworthy.
The first sin committed-
Some say Eve was guilty,
Adam loved her so-
He shared the pain she was feeling,
Both displeasing in God's eyes,
Began the cycle of a new way of life,
They felt ashamed covered their nakedness,
Hid in darkness-
Couldn't escape their father's sight.

From Genesis to Revelation-
I'm going to write me a reservation in the book of life- so on my judgment day they won't think twice.

There've been countless displays of mind-boggling miracles,
The ark of Noah and the great flood,
Sodom and Gomorrah two cities instantly destroyed,
Moses seemingly impossible mission to part the Red Sea,
Skeptics think it was a mystery,
Delivering thousands from captivity of Egyptian slavery,
David defeated Goliath with a single stone and slingshot,
Proving the bigger they are, the harder they fall,
Or merely believing in God can empower us all,
The greatest day ever Jesus the Messiah's birth,
Rather the day of His death,
Or should I say,
His resurrection three days later from where His body was left,
Accomplishing more in His life than the world's history all together,
Whether it was turning water to wine,
Or feeding five thousand with 5 loaves and 2 fish,
Healing the blind, crippled and sick,
Even walked on water,
Endured our pain, our shame, our problems, and sins,
While living His sinless life all the way down to the end,
The one way to salvation is through Him and only Him.

From Genesis to Revelation-
I'm going to write me a reservation in the book of life- so on my judgment day they won't think twice.

Now I must touch on the most important part of
    Christianity,
It's the central doctrine of understanding,
Three honorable entities the Father, the Son, and Holy
    Spirit each to be equal,
None greater or less than the other,
Yet together being one God,
Somewhat odd to those without knowledge,
Separate although distinct entities assimilated into
    Christian life and profession of faith,
A true miracle, too complicated for our minds to fathom,
The Father Jehovah, the Son Jesus, and the Holy Spirit,
A feeling you must experience to explain,
This is so serious the curious will think you're insane.

From Genesis to Revelation-
I'm going to write me a reservation in the book of life- so on my
    judgment day they won't think twice.

My Place

During the season of Lent,
I fell in love with someone else.

He loves me unconditionally,
So I must say "no" to you and "yes" to Him.

My body now belongs to HIM,
He has my heart-
He's all in my head.
This is how I will be fed.

There's still a place for you,
Now playing a spiritual tune.
I pray you find the melody to my new song.

Goodness

When I think about His goodness,
It takes me to a time,
Was down to my last dime.
Don't quite understand how He switched the detrimental plan,
Turned a dime into a grand.
There were situations I thought I couldn't handle,
Wanted to throw in the towel,
Yell surrender,
Yet, He reminded me of all the countless possibilities meant to be.
All foreseen dreams waiting to be released.

With Him

A smile was upon her chiseled doll face.
I could see in her eyes the favor and grace.
Her mold was specially crafted to spread love to those without it.
As she walks the path of her destiny with modesty,
Using her gifts-
To encourage,
To enhance,
To emphasize the powers from which it comes.
To be humane in a world that's insane.
She calls the name, Jesus.
With Him you shall overcome barriers in your way,
No matter how many you encounter a day.
Go forth and soar,
You are-
Destined to achieve,
Destined to lead,
Destined to impact this society.

Woman Behold Thy Son

I witnessed the demise of My Father's chosen kingdom
 through the seasons,
As tyranny ruled the nation needing regulations.
I volunteered to come,
We needed to find the one.
Searched wide,
Looked inside,
Chose you for Me to reside,
Sent Gabriel to abide,
To prepare you for glory on high.
I was there when Gabriel spoke with you,
Watched the Holy Spirit come upon you.
Your heart was pure,
Your soul was sure,
The chosen one to mother the Son.
You kissed My cheeks,
Held in your arms the Prince of Peace.
You followed My Father's plan as your hands nurtured
 Me to stand like a Man,
Savior of all the land.

Through My journey,
I traveled predestined roads to enlighten My Father's
 story,
To spread His glory.
I chose men to follow Me,
To witness miracles to be.
I healed the sick-
Crushed walking sticks,
Raised the dead-
Guided the misled,
Gave blind eyes sight-

Brought darkness to light,
Casted out spells-
Sent demons to hell,
Walked on water-
Saved sons and daughters.

Woman from whom I come behold thy Son,
His kingdom come,
His will be done as My blood runs-
The shade of red stains the sun.
The sky fades to black-
Thunder screams attack,
Clouds reveal their shields-
Lightning throws spears.
All of nature reacts-
Ready to battle on My command,
Be Still I say-
This is My Father's plan.

Woman why you weep at My feet,
This is meant to be.
I claim victory through agony,
My enemies shall remember then weep.
This cross is for all mankind,
Love,
Faith,
Peace will be left behind-
Seek thee shall find.

I want you to save your tears,
Cease your fears.
I recognize your hurt,
Sense your pain-
You must continue to proclaim My name.

I came to bear this cross,
The reason for My birth,
To save souls on earth.
This flesh withstood the test,
My Spirit shall fulfill the rest.
This is the beginning of My Holy meaning,
My disciples shall spread My teachings.
I shall return in three days,
Don't be afraid.
I shall transcend back to My home,
Sit on My throne,
Listen to angelic baritones.
Sshhh... I hear the seraphim's voices,
The celebration has begun.

Woman behold thy Son,
Disciples behold thy Mother,
I entrust you to care for Her like no other.

MBC

Morris Brown College

I Have a Revelation for MBC

I have a revelation,
One day Morris Brown College-
Will break through Her darkness,
She shall shine with a new beginning.

She will be placed amongst stars-
For all to witness Her glory and refining.

She stands on a foundation of history,
While She carries Her torch on proud shoulders-
Withstanding litigations,
Withstanding lies,
Withstanding financial challenges that are-
Hurled against Her from unconscious groups.
Yet, She continues to rise despite of tangled loops.

I have a revelation,
One day Morris Brown College will break down-
The tormented boundaries that overturned Her throne.

She retains Her pride as She continues to strive.
She shall sound Her chimes from the clock on Fountain
    Hall-
That tells Memoirs of Her time in remembrance of them
    all.

She shall empower minds,
Instill self-worth,
Nurture the young,
Tune the old,
Lead lost souls.

I have a revelation,
One day Morris Brown College will regain Her
    accreditation,
All closed doors shall open,
All stuttering tongues shall utter praises,
All critical eyes shall see Her resurrection.

I have a Revelation today,
We Must All Have A Revelation For Morris Brown
    College!

John H. Lewis Gymnasium

Long ago our forefathers paved roads to enrich hungry
    souls,
They were led by faith as they stood bold,
They listened for the swish of the Wolverines,
And over time felt their mighty sting,
Allowed their glory to ring in our beloved gym.

Upon the surface of the court,
Balls were dribbled to the goals, passed to untold souls,
Fumbled on once shining parquet floors,
Traveled during chimes of deadlines,
Reminders of class times.

Yes, we remember the shouts-
Rounds and abouts,
And the cheers that savored admiration in mid-air,
Unaware of defeats, or acts of retreats,
Affecting hearts of athletes to legacy links.

Beneath the surface lays countless dreams,
Swishing through mid-stream,
Awaiting opportunities to redeem.

There are still echoes of victory within the walls
    withstanding it all.
If you listen closely you can still hear the shouts-
Rounds and abouts.
Yes! The John H. Lewis Gymnasium must forever be
    etched in stones,
Up-keeping Morris Brown's legacy carved from our
forefathers' backbones.

Wilkes Hall

A place of rest is a nest where minds are restored.
The walls and halls drip sweat,
Due to endless study hours instilling power.
The effect flows from room to room,
Bonding students without gloom.
They gather in the common space,
As they trace backgrounds in an unfamiliar setting,
They fill the air contaminating nearby grounds with
    joyful sounds.
The bullhorn tells the history of the clock,
Most in shock,
From the lack of facts.
Of the historical school founded by former slaves,
Resting in their graves.
They embrace the intricacies as they continue to read,
They are bound by a higher power to stay on course,
Preserving the legacy without remorse.

Stance
(Louise T. Hollowell's Birthday Celebration)

Today we celebrate 104 years,
For the moments she shared in time as she destroyed
 barricades for decades.
The woman beside the man that took a stance,
She fought for civil rights with many demands.
She was the anchor for his existence-
The foundation for his steps.
She secured her hands with a holy grip-
To secure faith driven trips.
When she was not fighting for a civil case,
She taught in classrooms at distinguished Morris Brown
 College,
As a professor of English-
As she steered the youth in Fountain Hall with the
 foundation of truth.
Between those same walls she graduated amongst the top
 of her class,
She was determined to surpass,
Chose not to work in someone else's kitchen using a dish
 rag.
She was a beautician on Sweet Auburn Avenue,
She fine-tuned and groomed ladies in her salon,
Taught them to mend their sheer nylons.
Her legs were strong,
Toned beneath the bones,
As she stood against racism and oppression.

This is a celebration of dedication throughout the nation for those that took a stance without commemoration.

She knew from which she came from,
Walked proud as she stomped unjust grounds.
A queen that stood beside her king with honor,
Pride and dignity.
She stood beside Coretta when her husband freed Martin
 from Georgia's penitentiary.
She was a foot soldier for equal justice behind enemy
 lines,
Withstood the test of time through the trenches,
Sat on benches,
Tore down fences.
She was there in the court room–
When white college doors opened for black students
 classified as nuisances.
She was there when her husband made a fuss to keep us
 from the back of the bus,
She walked highways and byways for the sake of us.
There was purpose in her walk,
Power in her talk,
Love in her arms for her husband,
He charmed her for 61 years,
He made sure she was secure.
She shared the story of their love in a book "The Sacred
 Call"
His name engraved upon her heart on pages,
As she recorded their moments in time– in phrases.
She embraced the wise lines,
Brought forth power and pride,
She should truly be pleased with the legacy she leaves.

This is a celebration of dedication throughout the nation for those that took a stance without commemoration.

Who's the Man
(Math Professor Henry Porter)

Who's the man at Morris Brown,
That's known all over town?
Porter, Henry Porter… can you dig it!

Who's the man that gives a party,
Only for the student body?
Porter, Henry Porter… can you dig it!

Who's the man with a master plan,
That has volunteered for many years?
Porter, Henry Porter… can you dig it!

That Porter is a bad mother… shut your mouth. And nobody knows him but his wolverines.

Who's the man with all the charm,
That has a woman on each arm?
Porter, Henry Porter… can you dig it!

Who's the man that sings tenor,
That can hold a note as a soprano?
Porter, Henry Porter… can you dig it!

Who's the man that wears the Omega pin,
That's loyal through thick and thin?
Porter, Henry Porter… can you dig it!

That Porter is a bad mother… shut your mouth. And nobody knows him but his wolverines.

It's All about Helen
(Helen Kilpatrick Threatt's Celebration)

The Women for Morris Brown College are honoring
    their founder on this day,
A classy fashionable lady that paved this historical way.
The wife of the 12th President brought forth-
A distinguished group of women with shared purpose,
As their inner love surfaced in 1981,
To embrace the MBC legacy to infinity.
The young,
The wise,
The curious minds came to her beckoning,
To become members of this new happening.
They heard the astounding remarks from her pounding
    heart.

She aspired to promote a sense of pride,
Loyalty and support by her side,
Keeping the spirit of MBC alive.
During her reign-
She declared lines,
With dutiful signs.
She pioneered trails,
Launched sails,
Steamed rails through common grounds,
Brought aboard more charter members from around.

We celebrate her dedication of service,
As she offered everlasting merits.
Her ability to go beyond the mold-
To spread truths untold.
Now we thank you for endless thoughts of planning,

For making the Women for Morris Brown College
    outstanding.
On this day it's all about Helen,
As she poses with grace,
A smile upon her face,
Wearing her hat of taste.

Moments

If I Could Dance

Bill "Bojangles" Robinson paved the way for many dancers.
When I think about dancing,
I see silhouettes without faces,
Without races on a domain of places,
Striving toward a connection,
Trying to establish a relation,
So we can sway to the same destination.

If I could dance,
I would spread my arms as though they were wings.
I would soar toward heaven's door,
Touching little children in-between as they dream to empower them over many things.

If I could dance,
I would jump like Mr. Bojangles-
As he clicked his heels.
I would slide, glide, stride like the Nicholas Brothers-
As they moved to the sounds of Jumpin Jive by Cal Callaway-
On an unforgettable day.
I would entertain like Sammy Davis-
As a member of the Rat Pack-
Cause the Candy Man can.
I would bend, spin like Gregory Hines-
As he graced the stage on Broadway.
I would moonwalk like Michael Jackson-
As he captured the world's attention.

If I could dance,
I would quick step to the lyrics of "Yes We Can"-

By Will-I-Am to-
Justice, equality, prosperity.
I would mime to a new melody of "My Country 'Tis of
 Thee" sweet land of liberty–
Land where my father hung from a tree–
For me to be free.
I would stretch beyond to save sons from guns-
From shooting distant cousins.
I would teach young men to live beyond bars,
To remove battle scars.

If I could dance,
I would do a jazz strut to "Ain't Misbehavin"
On the floor of the Savoy.
A soulful motion to the beat of James Brown's-
"I Got Soul and I'm Super Bad."
A slow two step to the blues of Billie Holiday's-
"God Bless the Child that's got his own."
Stand on my toes in a concert hall with precise
 composition-
To a classical rendition by Lena Horne.

If I could dance,
I would dance like the freed Africans-
On this land to support my fellowman.
Tell my story through the rhythm that influenced the
 trend,
Made the blend of-
The Charleston,
The Lindy Hop,
The Jitterbug,
The Twist in this nation.

If I could dance,
I would lead lost souls-
From stained sheets-
To mountain peaks,
From I'm not my brother's keeper-
To I do know how to treat her,
From judicial brutality-
To self-reality.

If I could dance,
I would dance like King David with praise through a
    maze-
Provide consciousness to the dazed.
I would step in faith,
Turn-up my soul mate,
Leap to new heights,
Turn the economy around,
Move to-
Ah 1,
Ah 2,
Ah 3,
Ah 4,
While sliding smoothly across the floor through unjust
    doors.

If only I could dance-
Mr. Bojangles… Mr. Bojangles…
Dance, Dance, Dance,
If only-
I Could Dance…

What If

I stand for you to see who I am.
I knock on your open door to be sure.
I write and not speak just for you not to mistake my
 tone.
I want to make it right to avoid a fight.
To enhance plans taken from the wrong hands.
I can only walk with you not for you,
Our steps are not designed the same.
You see God made you differently than me,
Your flavor is distinct.

What if love dies,
Will you survive from the memories inside?
What if no rain falls,
Will your flowers bloom from unlost thoughts?
What if there's no common courtesy,
Yet you want mercy.
What if you depend on someone else to raise your child,
Will you change your profile?

Feel the intense passion without rations,
The explosion of diverse emotions with endless notions.
Paint a colorless canvas,
Use your imagination to create a place where we can
 relate.
I see us reaching, teaching, bringing meaningful
 meanings with the spirit of creative thinking for new
 beginnings.

What if you didn't know your history frow which you
 come,
Would you know your distant sons?

What if you didn't honor thy mother and father,
Will you have unmeasurable pleasure?
What if there was no government assistance,
Will there be children unfed within the system?
What if I don't abide,
Would you still call me friend,
Or would the relationship end?

Don't step to me if you're not ready to comprehend the
    mechanisms flowing beneath my skin.
I stand for you to see who I am.
I knock on your open door to be sure.

When

When I Wake
I seek opportunities to mend mistakes-
For His name's sake.

When I Pray
I kneel to keep from going astray,
To thank Him for another day,
To shape formless clay.

When I Dress
I press on layers to keep away distress,
To surpass His test.

When I Speak
I seek to defuse the inner me,
To defeat what buries the essence to be.

When I Praise
I raise the name of the Most High,
To magnify His glory,
To tell His story.

When I Look Back

I recall the story you told of the bond-
Between mother and son that formed in your womb,
As I listened to your tunes.
The songs you sang,
The diapers you changed,
The runny noses you wiped,
All with purpose and delight.

When I look back over my life,
I recall how you relieved me from strife,
How you endured sacrifice,
How you made everything alright.
The warm embrace to encourage me,
The kiss upon my head as we kneeled beside my bed.
To thank the Lord for another day,
To guard me as I lay,
To keep me safe through the night 'til the dawn of light.

Ashes to ashes, dust to dust, who am I to trust; ashes to ashes, dust to dust, to the one I love much.

When I look back over my life,
I recall the sternness you had to shape a man,
The love you gave to pave the way,
The wisdom for a future day.
The nourishment you fed my soul,
The possibilities of dreams unfold,
The provision to be bold,
The endurance to travel roads.

When I look back over my life,
I recall the day He called your name to meet His son,

He was ready for you, you obeyed.
You smiled with closed eyes as I stood by your side,
Placed the torch in my hand,
To pass to the next generation.
I thank God for placing me in your womb,
The bond between mother and son is like no other,
You instilled the purpose to live,
Yet you will always be remembered.

Ashes to ashes, dust to dust, who am I to trust; ashes to ashes, dust to dust, to the one I love much.

Voice
(Dedicated To Mom, Rosie L. Booker-Williams)

A distance away I hear a faint voice,
The sound of echoes carving remnants without a choice.
I try to understand the demands as they deepen.
I cover my ears to stop the source,
Realizing the sounds of recourse.
My heart expounds as the vibration of clarity is found,
A familiar voice softly whispers-
As I remember.

When she was young and free,
How she gave unconditionally.
When she fed the hungry,
Without the cost of money.
When she laughed,
Energized remorseful hearts to glad.
When she loved,
Gave soothing endless hugs.

She nurtured-
With her warm soup,
It nourished many through their loops.
She composed-
With her hands,
She extended them to keep others from sinking sand.
She encouraged-
With her tone,
She shared her home with those that roamed.
She was kind-
With her time,
She aided those with unclear minds.
My heart expounds as the vibration of clarity is found,

As she softly whispers-
I want you to remember.

Her voice fades as she walks away,
A gentle wind flows,
She turns and blows a kiss,
As tears of love grace my face.
At that moment I knew her message would instill her family in-place.
Generations to come shall know of her-
Bruised bent knees,
Noble deeds,
Planted seeds,
Bloom trees.
I shall savor the flavor of her stew,
The nourishment of morning dew.

Lost

My consciousness chimes,
I scatter to find the substance of my rhyme,
It's lost in time.

I scurry past the mirror in a justifiable hurry,
The reflection screams beyond means-
"IS IT ME- YOU'RE LOOKING FOR?"

Tonight there will be candles in windows,
Guiding shadows through meadows to soft pillows.
As lighthouses guide ships through misty waters solving
    tomorrow's problems.

Your Presence

For years we-
Worked,
Played,
And praised side by side,
Reaching mountain highs,
Shouting by and by,
'Til the morning rise.
We laughed together with tears in our eyes,
Filled with spiritual lullabies.
We validated with our hands to stand,
Talked of future plans,
Welcomed nomads,
While singing Glory Hallelujah extending our hands.
Your presence brought comfort,
Your eyes gave hope,
Your shoulders propelled strength,
Your image reflected worth,
While your heart loved unconditionally.
And you will always be so very special to me.
I pray the Most High God will cover you with His grace,
Position you in a serene place,
As you claim your new space,
With a smile upon your welcoming face.

Juneteenth

As the ship sailed to an unfamiliar land,
I then recalled my own native sand,
As the ocean waves raced us away to an unknown place.

I listened for the sounds of the drums from which I
 come from,
To keep me calm,
All I heard were moans and groans from my native sons.

The young and old sold for coins of gold,
Branded with hot metal, burned deep within their souls.

The backs of my king and queen from my native sand
 drooped before a white man,
Placed on an auction block with perplexed frowns,
Stripped from their crowns.
Once walked with broad proud backs,
Enslaved 'cause the color of their skin was black.

For centuries we were held bound,
President Lincoln signed the Emancipation
 Proclamation-
Freed most of the slaves around.
Not 'til General Granger rode into Galveston, Texas on
 June 19, 1865,
Freed the last of the slaves still held down.

Today we celebrate the freedom we have gained,
Give honor to our many brothers and sisters-
That endured the struggle and the pain.

Now "N" Then

Then is then,
Now is now,
What goes up must come down,
Once the young now the old,
That's the way the story goes.

Different time different flow-
The highs and the lows,
When Kurtis Blow rocked the show-
Now it's all about the swirl of the girls,
Hearing the whistles blow,
Dropping low to the beat of the show.

Though

Though I'm broken-
I face defeats with retreats yet complete.

Though I hover in the valley-
I claim the mountain peak as I seek.

Though I stand accused-
I call upon the Trinity to rid thine enemies.

Enough

Is when you walk away with only the clothes on your
    back,
Trembling with urgency to unknown expectancies.
With a child on your hip,
Another holding your fingertips.
Not having anywhere to go in a strange land,
Knowing in your heart the Most High God has a plan.
As you walk through the door,
You take your first step toward your destiny,
As foretold by the Trinity.
When enough is enough.

Once

Once young,
Now old,
Witnessed many dreams unfold.
Once afraid to speak,
Now courageous to aid the meek.
Once unwise,
Now read between dotted lines.
Once lost,
Now found,
Stand on hallow grounds,
Rebound sounds.
Once shallow,
Now mellow to loony tunes.
Once in despair,
Now purpose made aware,
Declaration to share,
Now beware.

I See

Life has a way of molding you without your knowledge,
Placing people around you to abide in this challenge.

It is not coincidental of the faces you see,
The ones you strangely meet.

Every action,
Every distraction used to prune you to satisfaction.

Your path led you to the roads passed by,
Not knowing why.

Some have been in your life longer than others,
There are some that are no longer.

Which means you got what you needed,
They served their purpose for the reason.

When I see you,
I see the essence of which you are to be,
There's something special within thee.

Each life you touched stands close by,
Will be by your side,
Will give you room to fly.

So go forth and soar,
Fly beyond,
Achieve your highest score.

They Fought

Think of the men of valor that loss their lives in foreign wars,
Leaving their loved ones on these soils.

They fought-
On land,
On sea,
Beyond boundaries of the clouds,
Now memoirs of history.

They fought for-
Freedom and social equality.

The victory of injustice and poverty for-
My country 'tis of thee-
The land of liberty,
Rid thee of inequity.

Let freedom truly ring-
Now sing a new meaning,
With an eruptible vast beginning.

They Have

They have…
Killed us with their hands
Used ropes, knives, tasers, guns on demand.
Killed us with their mouths
Used lies, false alibis, banged gavels to unravel woven
    lives.
Killed us with their eyes
Used unseen facts, impaired vision to reflect generational
    impact.
Killed us with their feet
Used boots to stomp dreams, crush off-springs to
    imprint unjust means.
Killed us with their minds
Used Willie Lynch plan to demoralized blood lines.
Now, they kill us with their knees
As we cry out we can't breathe.

We have…
Used our hands to build
Used our mouths to encourage
Used our eyes to visualize
Used our feet to strategize
Used our minds to rise
Used our knees to praise the Most High!
Now we demand justice in an unjust land.

Impact

The impact you made in my life was sanctioned,
Rationed,
Fashioned,
To exceed high expectations.

I recall the awkwardness,
Yet you held me sturdy.

I recall the nervousness,
Yet you graced me with a spirit of calmness.

I recall the uncertainties,
Yet you gave me assurance.

My time with you,
Designed to sharpen my insight,
To instill patience,
To develop awareness,
To appreciate your many attributes.

The moments were distinctively created,
To intertwine meaningful time.

You are the source of measures,
You assure others-
To obtain unclaimed treasures.

I Wish

If I could've talked to that younger me,
I would have kept her from pain,
Sorrow,
And shame.

I would have shown her how to praise His holy name,
To keep sane.

I would have told her of the many gifts she had inside,
Before she believed lies.

I would have taught her how to love herself,
To birth her worth,
To demise her hurt.

I would have looked into her eyes,
Told her the truth,
Held her hand to guide her through.

I wish she could have known,
What she knows now.

Bro-Man

When I looked into your eyes they pierced my soul,
I saw the past from which you come.
I was there with you before your hands were bound.
We wore crowns upon our heads,
Other heads bowed when we were around.
We once walked on the shore of our native land,
Hand in hand,
Our captures came with chains.
On that day on that shore were left many blood stains.
Separation brought us here to this land.
So please don't treat me as though you don't know me.

I felt every lash that struck your back,
As they tried to whip away your pride.
I saw the pain in your eyes as they raped me.
I endured the sounds of the guns as we were on the run.
We ran hand in hand through unfamiliar land for the
    sake of our unborn baby,
Cause you had a plan.
We ate the roots from the earth to keep alive,
Now you want to treat me unkind.
I am trying to understand Bro-Man why you treat me as
    though you don't know me.

I am the same woman that made sure we had a home,
I knew the struggles from which we come,
I remember your God given name.
I gave birth to your first son,
I cried with you when opportunities passed you by.
I felt your sorrow when you tried.

Together we have made it through-
The encounters of slavery,
The destructiveness of racism,
The division of segregation,
The lack of accreditation,
The oppression of to be generations.
So help me to understand Bro-Man the reason you lost sight of your plan.

I know what you have gone through,
Don't you remember?
I was there with you.
I held you tight through the night so you would be alright.
I wiped your tears as they fell on my pillow,
Now you speak to me as though I am shallow.
I searched through the soul of your eyes,
All I see is emptiness inside.
Your hands were once used to-
Protect me,
Guide me,
Caress me,
Now you raise them to strike me.
Your lips were used to kiss me,
Spoke words of kindness,
Now you use them to curse me.
Your eyes once sparkled at the sight of me,
Now they admire something different than me,
Which I do not understand.

I am really trying to make amends,
Where is the man I once knew,
Who said, "I will always love you?"
Where is the man that stood by my side when I cried?

Where is the man that would sacrifice his life for mine?
Now you walk with no pride,
Don't you know God is still by your side?
You have spent too many meaningless years that have
    caused you to lose your insight.
I need you to look into my eyes,
See the essence of what you should be.
You see,
The Most High is telling me-
I should not give up on thee.

Romance

Georgia Woman, Mississippi Man

On the soil of his grandfather comes a man,
He plays tunes,
Sings the blues,
Spoons the ladies with a smile.
I watch him from afar,
There're holes beneath his soles as he walks midair.
My heart skips a beat when he winks,
He caught my gaze-
Our shoulders engaged.
Or was I dazed from flashing rays?
Too soon to know the brightness of his moon,
The flavor from his spoon,
The scent of his upper room.
He grinds mid-stream,
Clings to routines,
Wipes his hands clean.

Georgia Woman, Mississippi Man,
Caught in the heart of this Delta land.
Too tough to handle,
Too hot to hold,
Too many blues beneath their souls.

On the soil of her grandfather comes a woman,
She binds truth,
Stays exclusive,
Spoons the men with her charm.
I watch her from afar,
There're scars upon her cheeks,
Her makeup lies beneath from heat,
As the audience stands to their feet.
From the east she flows,

To the west she goes,
Streaks to his motions with notions.
Echoes melodies,
Dances on legendary feet,
Sings beyond seats.
She grinds mid-stream,
Clings to routines,
Wipes her hands clean.

Georgia Woman, Mississippi Man,
Caught in the heart of this Delta land.
Too tough to handle,
Too hot to hold,
Too many blues beneath their souls.

Both caught in the moment,
Not allowing their tunes to bloom in June,
Too soon to smell the scents of their upper rooms.
Rain rinses away their names,
Two of the same,
No one to blame,
Caught in the moment,
Oh, what a shame.

Georgia Woman, Mississippi Man,
Caught in the heart of this Delta land.
Too tough to handle,
Too hot to hold,
Too many blues beneath their souls.

Love

When I was younger-
I abused and misused you-
Took advantage when you meant it.

When you detached yourself-
I often found you in the wrong places-
To fill empty spaces.

I used your name in vain-
Without shame.

The years have taught me to cherish you-
Now you refrain,
When I use your name "Love."

Is it Real

In the stillness of night,
I reach for you.
Feel nothing but space that was once your place.
I turn,
I sigh,
I'm terrified 'cause you're no longer by my side.
I gaze at the pillow where you laid your head,
Emptiness fills the bed.
I turn away from the empty space-
Where I kissed your sleeping face.
My gloom modulates to a jubilant tune-
As I think about the laughter of tales we told,
Love we made, as we witnessed dreams unfold.

Is it real, what's the deal, do you feel me?

I drift in and out of consciousness,
Visions of you appear,
Awake at half past eight.
I go throughout the day-
Thinking how we reached this position,
The terms of the condition-
Altered our mission.
Was our love not strong enough-
Did we surrender to fear-
Allow others with malice to influence our ears?
Or were we too afraid-
To interlock hearts like the locks on our heads,
Instead we dismissed the idea of wed-lock,
As we escaped the sound of the clock's tick tock in a
    state of shock.

Is it real, what's the deal, do you feel me?

I imagine us in a romantic setting on a patio deck,
You kiss me on the back of my neck,
We sway, we play, we lay in coolness of shade,
In the mid-day with motions of ocean waves.
I drift in and out of a hypnotic trance,
I feel your arms around my waist as we slow dance.
I touch your face, hold your hand,
We walk in a field with an array of lilies on a sloped hill,
Kiss underneath a waterfall,
Rest in a gold mine filled with priceless stones,
Sip red wine upon thrones,
Post pictures from our iPhones,
For all the world to see our innermost intimacies.

Is it real, what's the deal, do you feel me?

I search for memoirs of pleasures,
Infinite treasures of extreme measures.
I twice hear the tick tock of a clock,
Hit the snooze to continue the mood.
It was a dream within a dream,
Two souls lost in an illusion,
Came to a conclusion by unjustifiable confusion.
Or a prediction of foreseen depiction.
It is said,
Some lives are linked across the sands of time,
Now we must await our destiny with certainty.

Is it real, what's the deal, do you feel me?

Slow Dance

I like the way you use your hands on the keys,
I can only imagine how you can use them to appease me.

The tunes you play soothe my mood right away,
I want you to play a tune of love with me.

I want you to-
Stroke,
Hit,
Caress,
My heart,
My mind,
My soul,
From my toes to my nose.

I want my essence to respond,
You must go beyond-
Play a special melody upon.

I want to slow dance,
Feel the romance-
Lay in your arms tonight.
I want to hold you tight,
And flow to the moonlight.

We must guide our tunes to allow our flowers to bloom.
I want to feel every rhythmic heartbeat in the month of
    June.

I want to hear-
The sweet nothings whispered in my ear,
Taste the flavor of the word dear.

I want to look-
Into your eyes,
As your fingers orchestrate notes of harmony on strings of meaning.

I want to feel-
The intensity beyond my body,
I want to savor every stroke of high and low notes.

I want to slow dance,
Feel the romance-
Lay in your arms tonight.
I want to hold you tight,
And flow to the moonlight.

I Can't

No, I don't want you to love me,
I can't love you back,
There are zigzag lines between the cracks.

Not ready to jump the tracks,
Still mending this heart attack.

In fact,
I'm unsure how I would react,
I choose to stay intact.

He Will

Last night I had a vision of you kissing someone other
    than me,
As I wrestled between the sheets to be free.

I yearned for your touch.
That would be too much,
Instead I fell to my knees,
Asked God to give me strength with my celibacy.

Unconditional love flows from Him to me,
I know He will meet my every need.
He will set me free,
He will mend the broken seal,
He will make my dreams real.

Goodbye,
Don't cry,
Go sing a lullaby.

Hearts

My heart was numb for years,
I wouldn't allow it to feel,
Instead, I chose to make dreams real.

The rays from your stare pierced my soul.
Illuminations made known,
No hesitation to be told.

No time to waste.
Must make haste for our hearts' sake.

I've waited patiently for you my King,
Now our hearts sing a melody to future dreams.

Rhythms of the Heart

There were two different heartbeats that had different rhythms.
Wandering,
Searching,
Yearning-
To fill the emptiness they both had inside.
The two hearts had traveled across the same path many times,
Always beating on a different beat.
While crossing the two hearts heard a recognizable melody,
Began to dance to the rhythm of an enchanted beat.
The melody was simplistic,
Yet grand enough for a symphony.
Their hearts made a connection,
Not knowing they were predestined since their creation.
Neither heart had ever felt such completion,
Never experienced such a revelation.
As the hearts slowly danced,
They grew stronger-
And began to beat with the same rhythm.

I've been up and I've been down, I've had my heart tossed all around, but you're the only one for me.

The two hearts became one,
With that union they became inseparable.
The hearts had finally found-
The love they had yearned for,
The love they had searched for,
And the love they would die for.

You see,
Love will always find a way.
So come share my life,
Our love will last through all eternity,
Because I was nothing before you found the love in me.
Come stand beside me,
Not in front or behind thee,
But with me.

I've been up and I've been down, I've had my heart tossed all around, but you're the only one for me.

When mind boggling issues make us dance to an erratic beat,
Always remember how we danced to our first enchanted beat.
There will be times when our hearts have tears of joy and tears of pain,
You will still be the only one for me.
With the love I feel for you,
And the love you feel for me,
I know without a doubt our love will see us through,
For I am nothing without you.
As our hearts age through the years,
And the blood that goes a-coursing through our veins reach our aged,
But love filled hearts.
It will still be like the first time when our hearts danced to our first recognizable melody.

I've been up and I've been down, I've had my heart tossed all around, but you're the only one for me.